··· A **TIMELINE HISTORY** OF THE ···
MEXICAN-
AMERICAN WAR

·· **TIMELINE TRACKERS**: WESTWARD EXPANSION ··

ALISON BEHNKE

Lerner Publications ◆ Minneapolis

CONTENTS

Lerner Publications Company
A division of Lerner Publishing Group, Inc.
241 First Avenue North
Minneapolis, MN 55401 USA

For reading levels and more information, look up this title at www.lernerbooks.com.

Library of Congress Cataloging-in-Publication Data

Behnke, Alison.
    A timeline history of the Mexican-American War / Alison Marie Behnke.
        pages cm. — (Timeline trackers: westward expansion)
    Includes bibliographical references and index.
    Audience: Grades 4–6.
    ISBN 978-1-4677-8583-9 (lb : alk. paper) —
ISBN 978-1-4677-8638-6 (pb : alk. paper) —
ISBN 978-1-4677-8639-3 (eb pdf)
    1. Mexican War, 1846–1848—Juvenile literature.
I. Title.
E404.B44 2015
973.6'2—dc23   2015000953

Manufactured in the United States of America
1 – BP – 7/15/15

COVER PHOTO:
US general Winfield Scott leads his troops into Mexico City.

INTRODUCTION

In the early and mid-nineteenth century, the United States was a young country. It started as a small group of European colonies clustered on North America's eastern coast. After winning its independence, the nation grew quickly. And as its population and area increased, so did its ambitions.

US settlers soon headed westward. They sometimes moved onto lands that were not yet part of US territory. Much of this land—including Texas and California—belonged to Mexico. Then, starting with the Texas Revolution (1835–1836), conflict flared between the United States and Mexico. Those tensions would go on to ignite the Mexican-American War in 1846, which lasted almost two years. The war claimed thousands of lives. And it cost both countries millions of dollars. In the end, the United States won. Mexico lost a huge amount of land to its northern neighbor.

The war left behind two neighbors with a troubled past and a shared border. Since then Mexican Americans have sometimes found opportunity in the United States. They have also faced hardships and prejudice. And the ties between the United States and Mexico are strong, but not always simple. Those ties have important roots in the Mexican-American War.

TIMELINES

In this book, a series of dates and important events appear in timelines. Timelines are a visual way of showing a series of events over a time period. A timeline often reveals the cause and effect of events. It can help explain how one moment in history leads to the next. The timelines in this book display important turning points surrounding the Mexican-American War. Each timeline is marked with different intervals of time, depending on how close together events happened. Solid lines in the timelines indicate regular intervals of time. Dashed lines represent bigger jumps in time.

CHAPTER 1

NATIONS OF THE NEW WORLD

1521: Cortés's army defeats the Aztecs.

1600s: England forms colonies that will later become the United States.

1500   **1600**   **1700**   **1800**

1519: Hernán Cortés arrives in Mexico.

1535: Spain sets up a colonial government in Mexico.

1783: The United States wins independence from Great Britain.

The first people of Mexico began living there many centuries ago. Over thousands of years, Mexico was home to many groups of people. By the sixteenth century, the most powerful group was the Aztecs.

In the sixteenth century, Spanish explorers and soldiers began traveling to North, South, and Central America. Their goal was to conquer the region's peoples and claim the land for Spain. They also hoped to find gold and other riches in the New World. (Many Europeans at that time called the Americas the New World.)

One of the most famous Spanish soldiers was Hernán Cortés. He arrived in Mexico in 1519. By 1521 Cortés and his troops had defeated the Aztecs. Spanish forces killed thousands and forced many others into slavery.

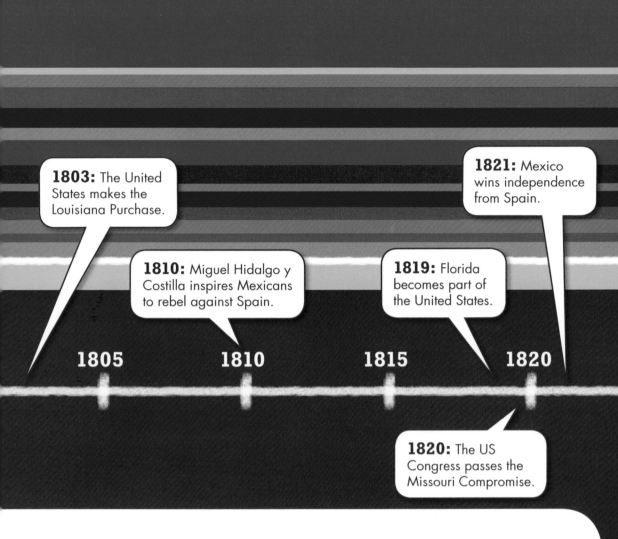

1803: The United States makes the Louisiana Purchase.

1810: Miguel Hidalgo y Costilla inspires Mexicans to rebel against Spain.

1819: Florida becomes part of the United States.

1821: Mexico wins independence from Spain.

1805   1810   1815   1820

1820: The US Congress passes the Missouri Compromise.

After Cortés's victory, Spain claimed Mexico as its own territory. In 1535 Spain set up a colonial government in Mexico. Colonists forced European customs on the people they had defeated. One of the main ideas Spain sent to the New World was its religion, Catholicism. Spanish missionaries in Mexico worked to convert the native peoples to this branch of Christianity.

A Growing Neighbor

Spain was not the only nation to send explorers and settlers to North America. Beginning in the early seventeenth century, settlers from England formed colonies along the eastern coast of North America.

Over time, many colonists began to disagree with British rulers. After the American Revolutionary War (1775–1783), the colonists won their independence from Great Britain.

The young United States quickly expanded southward and westward. In 1803 the country gained a huge amount of land when the United States bought the Louisiana Territory from France. The United States paid $15 million for the vast region west of the Mississippi River. The Louisiana Purchase nearly doubled the area of the United States.

At times the United States competed with Spain for land.

THE SPARK OF REVOLUTION

On September 16, 1810, Miguel Hidalgo y Costilla, a Catholic priest, gave a speech in the town of Dolores. This speech became known as the Grito de Dolores, or "the Cry of Dolores." Hidalgo called for his fellow Mexicans to rebel against the Spanish. He is honored as the father of Mexico's independence movement. In 1811 the Spanish captured and killed Hidalgo. But his words had fanned the flame of rebellion.

Spain controlled Florida, but for decades US leaders tried to add it to the United States' territory. One way the nation did this was by encouraging US citizens to settle in Florida. In 1810 US settlers in Florida rebelled against Spanish rule, and on February 22, 1819, Spain and the United States signed the Adams-Onís Treaty. This agreement gave Florida to the United States in exchange for $5 million.

The Adams-Onís Treaty also defined the border between Mexico and the United States. Spanish and US leaders had argued about this border ever since the Louisiana Purchase. In particular, they disagreed about who controlled parts of Texas. According to the treaty's terms, Texas officially belonged to Spain.

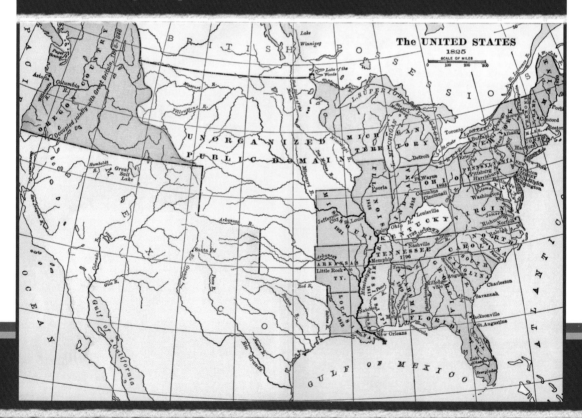

The Adams-Onís Treaty of 1819 defined which territory belonged to the United States and which belonged to Spain.

Rebellion

Meanwhile, many Mexicans had grown tired of Spanish rule. In the colony, Spanish-born people held most of the power and the money. The next most powerful group was the criollos, people of Spanish descent who had been born in Mexico. Further down the ladder were the mestizos, who were descended from marriages between Spanish colonists and native peoples. Native peoples held the least power in Mexican society.

Many Spanish-born colonists wanted to cut ties with the Spanish government and form an independent nation. Meanwhile, many criollos and others thought that people born in Mexico should govern, free from Spanish rule. Though these groups disagreed on who should be in power, they agreed that Mexico should break away from Spain. Tensions mounted. After a decade of struggle, Mexico won its freedom from Spain in 1821.

President James Monroe

President Monroe Speaks His Mind

On December 2, 1823, President James Monroe gave his State of the Union Address, the president's yearly speech to the US Congress. He talked about the relationship between Europe and the Americas. The United States wanted to protect its land and its borders from any European attempts to form new colonies.

Monroe said that if European nations tried to claim lands anywhere in the Western Hemisphere, the United States would view those actions as a direct threat. The nation could choose to respond to that threat with force. On the other hand, Monroe said, as long as Europe did not cause trouble for the United States, the United States would not interfere in European affairs. This philosophy became known as the Monroe Doctrine.

A DEEP DIVIDE

As the United States grew, its gains in territory sparked debates over other issues—especially slavery. In southern states, slavery was legal. Enslaved people of African descent were forced to work in fields and homes. Most lived in terrible conditions. Many northern states had outlawed slavery, and some northerners wanted slavery outlawed nationwide. Southerners resisted, saying states should decide for themselves. And in the US Congress, leaders wanted the number of slave states and free states to be the same. That way, political power would be spread evenly between the two sides.

In 1820 Congress passed the Missouri Compromise to address the slavery question. This law said that Missouri would enter the nation as a slaveholding state. And Maine would enter as a free state, keeping an equal balance between free states and slave states. The law included a plan for the huge Louisiana Territory. It defined a boundary running through the new territory from east to west. North of this line, slavery would be illegal.

CHAPTER 2

THE ROAD TO WAR

1830: Mexico closes Texas to foreign immigration.

1815   1820   1825   1830

1824: The Santa Fe Trail becomes an important trade route between the United States and Mexico.

In the early nineteenth century, many US citizens were moving west, looking for better lives and bigger opportunities. The West offered great potential for farming, logging, hunting, and mining.

Some settlers crossed the border into Texas, which was part of Mexico. After winning its independence, Mexico was working to set up its government and laws. Mexican leaders wanted people to settle the areas along the Mexico–US border. They were worried that the United States might want to claim Mexican territory, and they believed that border settlements would help protect the land from being taken over.

In 1823 Texas was not a comfortable place for new settlers. It was far from the capital, Mexico City. Only about twenty-five hundred to thirty-five hundred Mexicans lived in the region. But

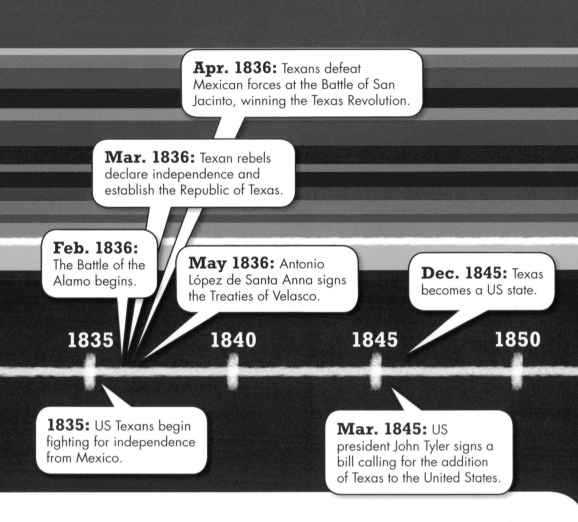

Apr. 1836: Texans defeat Mexican forces at the Battle of San Jacinto, winning the Texas Revolution.

Mar. 1836: Texan rebels declare independence and establish the Republic of Texas.

Feb. 1836: The Battle of the Alamo begins.

May 1836: Antonio López de Santa Anna signs the Treaties of Velasco.

Dec. 1845: Texas becomes a US state.

1835   1840   1845   1850

1835: US Texans begin fighting for independence from Mexico.

Mar. 1845: US president John Tyler signs a bill calling for the addition of Texas to the United States.

Texas was also home to several thousand American Indians. These independent nations had been in the area for many generations. When Mexican settlers arrived, they brought threats to the cultures and even the lives of native peoples. Sometimes Mexican settlers killed American Indians or forced them into slavery. In response to these threats, groups of American Indians sometimes attacked settlements and robbed or killed Mexican settlers.

Mexican leaders passed laws allowing foreign settlers to buy land in this region and become Mexican citizens. The Mexican government hoped these settlers would protect the border. Thousands of US settlers responded eagerly to the chance. Land in Texas cost less money than land in the United States. In addition, slavery was legal in the region. This attracted settlers who wanted to own slaves.

US settlers were also moving to the Mexican-owned territories of New Mexico and California. In New Mexico, the city of Santa Fe was an important trading outpost. Residents were eager to buy goods from the United States. Beginning in 1824, merchants traveled along the Santa Fe Trail, which ran to New Mexico from Franklin, Missouri.

Texas Revolts

By the end of the 1820s, Mexican leaders had a problem. So many US settlers had moved to Texas that they outnumbered the Mexican residents. So in 1830, Mexico's president, Anastasio Bustamante, declared that he would not allow any more US immigrants to settle in Texas.

Mexican leaders were right to be concerned. US settlers in Texas sometimes challenged Mexican laws. For instance, when Mexico outlawed slavery in 1829, the practice continued in Texas. As time went on, the issue created further friction between Mexico's government and US-born Texans.

Mexican leaders tried to tighten their control over the Texas frontier. But Texans pushed back. In the autumn of 1835, US settlers in Texas began a fight for independence. The first clashes of the Texas Revolution took place in October.

Remember the Alamo

In December 1835, Texans took control of San Antonio. The Mexican Army, led by Antonio López de Santa Anna, arrived in February 1836 to take back the city. The small Texan force gathered at the Alamo, an old Spanish mission in San Antonio.

Mexican troops had used the Alamo as a fort in the past. It had tall, thick walls and was armed with cannons. The Texans who gathered there hoped they could defend the Alamo long enough for their fellow rebels in other parts of Texas to send help.

The Battle of the Alamo began on February 23. Santa Anna's troops surrounded the fort and battered the walls with gunfire and cannonballs. Santa Anna had about eighteen hundred troops—roughly ten times more men than the Texans. The Alamo's defenders kept waiting for help from outside. But fewer than one hundred men arrived.

The siege lasted for twelve days. Then, on the thirteenth day, Santa Anna ordered his soldiers to storm the Alamo. Before sunrise on March 6, the Mexican troops charged the Alamo and managed to get inside. A fierce battle followed inside the Alamo's walls. When the fighting was over, the Texans had been badly defeated. Santa Anna's troops had killed almost everyone in the fort.

Mexican troops storm the Alamo, overpowering the small number of Texans defending the fort.

A few weeks later, Santa Anna's men captured Texan soldiers near the town of Goliad. At Santa Anna's order, all the prisoners—more than three hundred men—were executed.

The losses at the Alamo and at Goliad upset many people in Texas and the United States. In response, a wave of people pledged to join the Texans in their fight against Mexico. They were inspired by the battle cries, "Remember Goliad!" and "Remember the Alamo!"

Antonio López de Santa Anna

From Republic to State

While the Battle of the Alamo raged, Texan leaders met to talk about the future. They issued a declaration of independence on March 2, 1836. This document officially created the Republic of Texas.

The Texas Revolution's last battle was on April 21, 1836, at San Jacinto. The Texan forces were outnumbered again. But this time, the Texans won. Texan leader Sam Houston took Santa Anna as a prisoner. On May 14, Santa Anna signed the Treaties of Velasco. These treaties said that Texas had won its independence.

But Mexican leaders refused to recognize the Treaties of Velasco. They claimed that Santa Anna did not have the right to represent the Mexican government, so his signing of the treaty was meaningless. Meanwhile, some US leaders—including President John Tyler—hoped to claim Texas as part of US territory. Support for this idea increased in 1844 when James K. Polk was elected to follow Tyler. On March 1, 1845, before leaving office, Tyler signed a bill that called for the United States to take control of Texas.

By then the United States was one of the largest countries in the world. Texas was a relatively small republic pinned between two much bigger nations. Many Texans felt that joining the United States was their smartest move. So on June 16, 1845, the Texas Congress agreed to this plan. On December 29, Texas became the country's twenty-eighth state.

MANY NATIONS

The regions that the United States and Mexico would fight over in the Mexican-American War were home to thousands of American Indians. They had lived on the land for many generations. They formed many separate, independent groups, sometimes called nations. In California those groups included the Yuma, the Chumash, the Cahuilla, the Pomo, and many others. In parts of New Mexico and Arizona, some of the major nations were the Pueblo, Zuni, Navajo, and Hopi peoples. Nevada, Utah, and southwestern Kansas and Colorado were home to Shoshone, Paiute, Goshute, and Ute peoples, while the Apache, the Comanche, and other groups lived in Texas. Each of these groups had distinct customs and cultures. Some lived in settled villages, while others were nomadic. Some raised crops, and others excelled at hunting. Their religion, government, dress, and diet varied. But all would be affected by the conflict between Mexico and the United States.

CHAPTER 3

THE FUSE IS LIT

July 1845: US president James K. Polk orders General Zachary Taylor to gather troops in Corpus Christi, Texas.

May 1846: US and Mexican troops fight the Battle of Palo Alto. A few days later, the US Congress officially declares war against Mexico.

JUNE 1845   **SEPT. 1845**   **DEC. 1845**   **MAR. 1846**

Nov. 1845: Polk sends John Slidell to Mexico to buy California and New Mexico.

Despite US claims, Mexican leaders still insisted that Texas remained part of Mexico.

Mexico and the United States also disagreed on where Texas's southern border was. According to the United States, the border was a river called the Rio Grande. But Mexico argued that the Nueces River, north of the Rio Grande, had always been the true border between Texas and the rest of Mexico. Even if Texas eventually became part of the United States, Mexico demanded that the Nueces be recognized as the border. As these disputes dragged on, tensions ran high between the two countries.

Polk prepared to fight for Texas. He also hoped to take control of New Mexico and California. And he believed that in the face of US military might, Mexico would agree to sell

July 1846: US Navy commander John Sloat and his troops occupy Monterey, California.

Aug. 1846: Kearny and his army take control of New Mexico for the United States.

JUNE 1846   **SEPT. 1846**   **DEC. 1846**   **MAR. 1847**

June 1846: US settlers in California revolt against Mexican control. Stephen Kearny leads his troops toward New Mexico.

Jan. 1847: The conflict in California ends, and the United States claims the region.

this land for a good price. So in July 1845, he ordered US Army general Zachary Taylor to gather troops in Corpus Christi, Texas. Polk sent another military leader, Commodore David Conner, to prepare ships in the Gulf of Mexico.

A few months later, in November, Polk sent Congressman John Slidell to Mexico on a mission to meet with Mexican leaders. Slidell would offer to buy New Mexico for $5 million and California for $25 million. He would also try to settle the question of the US-Mexico border. But Mexican leaders were not eager to negotiate with the United States. Top officials refused to meet with Slidell. Slidell reported the news to Polk and added that force might be the only way for the US leaders to get what they wanted.

Into the Nueces Strip

Polk responded to Slidell's news by ordering General Taylor to begin moving his army south toward the Rio Grande. Polk claimed that if Mexico refused to negotiate, the only option would be for the United States to declare war. Polk referred to the Monroe Doctrine to back up his claim. Since Mexico was free of European control, Polk's argument stretched the limits of the Monroe Doctrine. But many US leaders agreed with Polk's plans.

In March, with no further progress, Polk ordered Taylor and his troops into the Nueces Strip. This area between the Rio Grande and the Nueces River was exactly the region that Mexico said would remain Mexican territory even if the Treaties of Velasco were accepted.

Mexico viewed this as a hostile act by the United States. It sent troops toward the Rio Grande. The Mexican Army gathered on the other side of the river at the town of Matamoros. On April 25, General Mariano Arista instructed a group of his soldiers to cross the Rio Grande into the Nueces Strip. Taylor ordered a smaller group of his own men to meet the Mexican party. Arista's troops surrounded the US soldiers,

General Mariano Arista

killed and wounded several men, and captured the rest.

This clash was the spark that set off the war. Taylor sent Polk a message telling him that the fighting had begun. Polk then urged Congress to declare war against Mexico. After a short debate, both the House of Representatives and the Senate voted to go to war. On May 13, 1846, the United States officially began the Mexican-American War.

Many miles away, the war was already being fought. On May 8, US and Mexican troops had had their first major battle. The Battle of Palo Alto took place along the road to Matamoros. US troops were outnumbered, but their guns had a longer range than those of the Mexicans. By the end of the day, Mexican troops had suffered far more losses than the US side. They retreated, and the US commanders claimed victory.

The very next day, the armies faced each other again at the Battle of Resaca de la Palma. Once again, the US troops proved stronger. Many Mexican soldiers were killed. In confusion and fear, Arista's troops fled back across the Rio Grande.

The Battle of Palo Alto was one of the first battles between US troops and Mexican troops.

Soon Arista and his men retreated from Matamoros. They hoped to regroup deeper in Mexican territory. On May 18, Taylor's forces occupied Matamoros.

California Crisis

Unrest was also stirring in the Mexican territory of California. In June 1845, the US government had sent John C. Frémont and a small group of US troops to California. Frémont told Mexican officials that he was only there to explore the region. But then, in June 1846, a small group of US settlers launched a revolt against Mexican control in California. Frémont and his men quickly gave support to these rebels. The settlers declared part of California an independent republic. They wrote a constitution and created a homemade flag featuring a grizzly bear. The flag gave the rebellion a name: the Bear Flag Revolt.

The revolt in California was a sign of Mexico's weakening control in the area. And the United States was prepared to take advantage of that. Also in June, the US government ordered Colonel Stephen W. Kearny to lead an

The homemade flag of the Bear Flag Revolt featured a grizzly bear.

army westward. Kearny's mission was to claim New Mexico and California for the United States.

Kearny's troops headed to New Mexico first. They reached the city of Santa Fe in August. Many residents of New Mexico were willing to accept US rule. They were unhappy with the Mexican government. And they knew that if it came to a battle, the US troops would easily defeat the region's smaller Mexican force.

As the US troops approached, the Mexican governor of New Mexico abandoned the area with his army. A few days after arriving in New Mexico, Kearny's troops raised the US flag over Santa Fe's main plaza. They hadn't even fired a shot. Within a few weeks, Kearny moved on to California.

Kearny and his troops raise the US flag over Santa Fe, New Mexico.

While Kearny marched westward, another US commander had been preparing to help claim California. Commodore John Sloat led the US Pacific Squadron, part of the US Navy. In July Sloat and his troops landed at Monterey, on the coast of California. They swiftly occupied the town.

Commodore John Sloat

Sloat delivered a message to the people of Monterey—both US settlers and people of Mexican descent, called Californios. Sloat's message promised these people all the rights and protections of US citizens. The Bear Flag rebels pledged their loyalty to the United States. Sloat's troops moved on to occupy San Francisco.

Later in July, Robert Stockton took over command from Sloat and got ready to move south. Stockton's goal was Los Angeles. There, Mexican officials once more saw that their forces could not compete with US troops. They surrendered immediately. Stockton occupied the town in mid-August.

Several minor clashes followed in the fall. Californios tried to force out the US troops. In Los Angeles, Californio fighters succeeded in forcing the surrender of US troops. Then, in December 1846, Kearny reached California with some of his soldiers. On December 6, at the valley of San Pasqual, Kearny's men attacked a group of Mexican forces. Kearny's exhausted men had just marched 2,000 miles (3,218 kilometers) from Santa

Fe. At first it seemed the Mexicans would overpower the weary US troops. But when US reinforcements arrived, the Californios retreated. Kearny claimed victory, though he had suffered heavy losses. His remaining troops moved on to San Diego.

The last battles in California took place in January 1847. After winning the Battle of San Gabriel River, US troops marched back to Los Angeles on January 10. They officially occupied the city once more. On January 13, John Frémont and Mexican commander Andrés Pico signed the Treaty of Cahuenga. The agreement formally ended the conflict in California and claimed the region for the United States.

POPULAR OPINION

US citizens had mixed opinions about the war with Mexico. Some who supported the war believed the United States had the right—and even the responsibility—to settle and own land in North America. This idea is sometimes called manifest destiny. It was partly rooted in racism, which was common in the United States. Many white Americans were prejudiced against people with darker skin, including Mexicans and native peoples. These white people believed they should have access to more land, more wealth, and more opportunities than other groups of people.

Other people in the United States were against the war. Opponents of slavery did not want to add more territory to the southern United States. According to the Missouri Compromise, most of these new regions could become slaveholding areas. Critics of the war also said the conflict was an unjust use of power against a weaker neighbor. Antiwar figures included famous writers Henry David Thoreau and Frederick Douglass.

CHAPTER 4

TOWARD MEXICO CITY

Apr. 1847: The Battle of Cerro Gordo ends with a US victory.

Feb. 1847: The Battle of Buena Vista takes place.

SEPT. 1846   NOV. 1846   JAN. 1847   MAR. 1847   MAY 1847

Sept. 1846: US general Zachary Taylor and his forces reach Monterrey, Mexico.

Mar. 1847: US troops win the Battle of Veracruz.

While US forces took control of California, the war to the south continued. General Zachary Taylor had orders to move deeper into Mexican territory. In the long term, the US goal was to take the capital, Mexico City. But that was many miles away from Matamoros, the army's current location. For Taylor the next target was the town of Monterrey, Mexico.

The Journey South

In late September 1846, Taylor and his forces reached Monterrey. They faced off against Mexican forces led by General Pedro de Ampudia. The Mexican troops had built forts and prepared the city for the US attack. Ampudia had more than seven thousand men. The US side had about six thousand US soldiers.

Aug. 1847: US general Winfield Scott's troops fight two battles near Mexico City.

Jan. 1848: Nicholas Trist negotiates terms to end the Mexican-American War.

JULY 1847   SEPT. 1847   NOV. 1847   JAN. 1848   MAR. 1848

Sept. 1847: US forces occupy Mexico City.

Feb. 1848: The United States and Mexico sign the Treaty of Guadalupe Hidalgo.

Mexican troops defend a fort in Monterrey, Mexico, against US attack.

US troops attacked Monterrey from two sides. When most Mexican troops moved farther into the town's center, US forces began going from house to house. They threw explosives into homes, chasing out soldiers hiding there. Taylor's forces moved closer and closer to the town's main plaza. The church on the plaza sheltered many townspeople. It also held much of Ampudia's ammunition. Finally, as the US troops closed in on the plaza, the town's last major stronghold, Ampudia surrendered. US forces took control of the city on September 25.

The next big conflict for Taylor's troops was in February 1847. The Battle of Buena Vista began on February 22. Mexico's troops were once again under the command of Antonio López de Santa Anna. Hearing that Taylor's troops were headed south, Santa Anna moved to attack.

The battle took place in a narrow valley. Taylor's troops were vastly outnumbered. But the US side had several advantages. They had powerful weapons, and they also had

The Battle of Buena Vista

a good position in the valley. In addition, Santa Anna made a key mistake in leading his soldiers. He began a retreat just when the Mexican troops seemed on the verge of victory. By the morning of February 24, Mexican troops had fled. Many US soldiers were dead. Yet despite huge odds, Taylor had won his last major clash of the war. Northern Mexico was under US control.

A KEY FIGURE RETURNS

Antonio López de Santa Anna had a long and complicated history with Mexico—and with the United States. He helped overthrow multiple leaders, and he held the Mexican presidency several times himself. Santa Anna was also a military hero to many Mexicans, in part for his role in the Battle of the Alamo. US troops, on the other hand, saw him as ruthless.

Santa Anna's fifth term as president began when he led a coup to overthrow the government in 1841. But he pushed his power too far, and his dictatorial rule angered many. With opinion rising against him, he went into exile in Cuba in 1845.

But Santa Anna did not give up easily. He wanted to return to Mexico. So when the Mexican-American War erupted, he persuaded Mexico's government to allow him back into the nation to help them fight off the American invaders. After all, he'd shown his worth in battle before.

To reach Mexico, however, Santa Anna also had to get past the US military ships blocking his way. He managed to convince Polk to allow him through, saying that he'd use his influence with Mexican leaders to negotiate peace on terms that would be good for the United States.

But once he was back on Mexican soil, Santa Anna broke his promises to both nations. He seized control of the Mexican government yet again. Then, as commander of the Mexican Army, he led troops against the US powers he'd formerly pledged to help.

Veracruz and Beyond

While Taylor moved south, Polk had ordered General Winfield Scott to attack the port of Veracruz on Mexico's eastern coast. From there, Scott planned to advance to Mexico City.

On March 9, 1847, US troops landed on a beach just south of Veracruz. The next day, they began a siege of the city. This time, the Mexican forces were outnumbered. But Veracruz was surrounded by a wall and several forts. Scott's troops circled the city, cutting off access to food, water, and other supplies. On March 22, Scott urged Mexican troops to surrender. They refused. So Scott's men bombarded Veracruz with gunfire for two days. Many civilians died along with soldiers. Finally, on March 27, the city surrendered.

Fight to the Finish

After the victory at Veracruz, Scott began marching to Mexico City. Near the town of Cerro Gordo, the road to the capital led

US troops invade the port of Veracruz on Mexico's eastern coast.

through a narrow pass. Scott's troops reached the pass in mid-April. And Santa Anna was waiting with his army.

Santa Anna had a good position and thousands of troops. His men blocked the road and took up posts in the hills. But one of Scott's officers, Captain Robert E. Lee, found a way to get around Santa Anna's troops. Some US soldiers attacked from the front, while others took Lee's path and struck from behind. Surprised and alarmed, Santa Anna and many of his men fled. When the battle ended, US troops had seized the road leading straight to Mexico City.

By mid-May, Scott's troops had set up camp in the town of Puebla, about halfway between Veracruz and Mexico City. But many of Scott's soldiers had reached the end of their service time. Instead of signing up for months more of fighting, two to three thousand men headed home. Scott needed more troops before heading to Mexico City. Yet Polk was slow to send more men.

The Battle of Cerro Gordo

But Polk did send Nicholas Trist. His job was to meet with Mexican officials and convince them to sign a treaty. Polk wanted this peace agreement to grant large amounts of land to the United States.

While Trist tried to get a meeting with Santa Anna, Scott planned his march to Mexico City. More troops had finally arrived. In August 1847, US forces entered the Valley of Mexico. Once again, Santa Anna was ready. He had an army of thirty-six thousand men to defend Mexico City.

On August 20, the armies fought two battles just south of the capital. The first was the Battle of Contreras. Santa Anna made another key mistake in commanding his soldiers. He retreated when he could have fought back and maybe even won. The fighting lasted just seventeen minutes. The Mexican side suffered major losses.

From Contreras, Santa Anna drew back to Churubusco. This would be the site of the day's second battle. Both sides fought hard and lost many men, but the US troops seized another victory.

General Winfield Scott (*on horseback*) led US troops to victory at the Battle of Contreras.

To the Gates of the Capital

With peace still out of reach, Scott had just one prize left in his sights. The capital was only a few miles away. In early September, US troops launched the Battle of Mexico City.

Before they could reach the city itself, Scott's men faced two challenges just outside town. The first was El Molino del Rey. This group of stone buildings was guarded well. But US troops managed to get inside El Molino. Mexican troops had to surrender.

The next step on the way to Mexico City's gates was Chapultepec Castle. This military school was perched on top of a hill. On September 12, US forces began firing on the castle. The assault lasted all day. The next day, troops attacked the castle from two sides at once. Scott's men stormed the hill and broke through the walls. The Mexican troops fought fiercely, but they just couldn't hold the castle. US forces claimed victory.

The Chapultepec Castle in modern-day Mexico City

On September 14, Scott's men marched into Mexico City. The troops occupied the capital and claimed it for the United States. But peace did not immediately follow. Although Mexico City's conquest marked the war's final battle, no treaty had been signed. That meant the conflict was not truly over. After death and suffering on both sides, many people wanted an official end to the war.

Nicholas Trist had continued to negotiate with Mexican officials. In late 1847 and early 1848, he finally made some

THE SAN PATRICIOS

One unique group of soldiers fighting for Mexico was Saint Patrick's Battalion (known in Spanish as the San Patricios). This group was made up of Catholic immigrants who had moved to the United States. Most had come from Ireland. Others were German or English. These men had been members of the US Army. But they faced discrimination and prejudice in the United States because of their religion. (Most commanders in the US military were Protestants. In Mexico, however, Catholicism was the main religion.) Several hundred of these Catholic immigrants deserted the US forces and joined the Mexican side of the conflict. These soldiers were knowledgeable about US weapons and strategies. They played a key role in the Battle of Buena Vista. Nevertheless, the Mexican troops ultimately lost that battle, and later many of the San Patricios were killed in the fighting. Others were captured by US forces. Some of the captured soldiers were executed for treason. The rest were severely punished.

The San Patricios were just a small force, and their service had little effect on the war's outcome. But they were honored in Mexico as heroes, while US leaders considered them traitors. Their place in history—like many aspects of the Mexican-American War—is seen very differently north and south of the US-Mexico border.

progress. By January 1848, the two sides had reached a deal. The United States pledged to pay Mexico $15 million in return for control of New Mexico and California. And Mexico finally agreed to set the Texas–Mexico border at the Rio Grande. Mexicans who lived north of this border could become US citizens if they wished. Otherwise, they could move south and remain Mexican citizens. The treaty promised that those who stayed would be able to keep their land.

On February 2, both sides signed a treaty accepting these terms. It was called the Treaty of Guadalupe Hidalgo. The document was quickly sent to Washington, DC. In March the US Senate ratified the treaty. In May, Mexican lawmakers did the same. At long last, the Mexican-American War had ended.

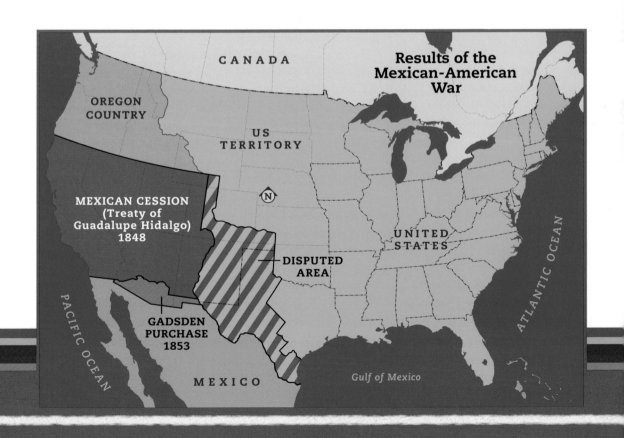

CHAPTER 5

NEIGHBORS

1846–1848: The US Congress considers and votes against the Wilmot Proviso.

Sept. 1850: The US Congress passes the Compromise of 1850.

1858–1861: Mexico fights the War of Reform.

1845   1850   1855   1860   1865

Jan. 1848: Gold is discovered in California.

1861–1865: The United States fights the Civil War.

The Mexican-American War left behind deep scars. More than 12,500 US troops were dead. Thousands more were wounded. At least 25,000 Mexican soldiers and civilians had been killed. And fighting had shattered many towns in Mexico.

The United States had gained vast lands from the conflict. Over time, these lands would make up much of California and New Mexico. They also formed parts of Nevada, Utah, Arizona, Oklahoma, Kansas, Colorado, and Texas.

The Treaty of Guadalupe Hidalgo promised fair treatment and equal rights to Mexicans who became US citizens. But in reality, Mexican Americans faced widespread prejudice and discrimination. In addition, the US government did not honor its promise that all Mexican Americans would keep their land.

1962: Cesar Chavez and Dolores Huerta found the United Farm Workers labor union.

1910–1920: The Mexican Revolution occurs. Mexican immigration to the United States increases dramatically.

1939–1945: World War II takes place.

1910   1920   1930   1940   1950

1929: The League of United Latin American Citizens is founded. The Great Depression begins.

1942: The Bracero Program begins.

The Battle of Veracruz left lasting destruction throughout the Mexican town.

In the mid-nineteenth century, many white citizens were moving west. They urged US leaders to let them claim land belonging to Mexican American families.

California's gold rush increased this pressure. Settlers had found gold in California in January 1848. Soon thousands of white settlers moved west to seek their fortunes. Many moved onto land that belonged to Mexican Americans. The government agreed to transfer land rights to these new settlers. Similar transfers took place in New Mexico and Texas.

Well after the war's end, the United States and Mexico still disagreed over one piece of territory: the Mesilla Valley. In modern times, the area is in southern Arizona and New Mexico. In 1853 US president Franklin Pierce sent ambassador James Gadsden to Mexico to settle the question. Mexico agreed to sell the area to the United States for $10 million. The deal was called the Gadsden Purchase.

Surveyors mapped out territory that Mexico would sell to the United States as part of the Gadsden Purchase.

Wars North and South of the Border

Not long after the Mexican-American War drew to a close, both the United States and Mexico faced growing unrest from within.

In Mexico, tensions between different political parties had simmered since the early nineteenth century. In the aftermath of the Mexican–American War, these different groups had different ideas for how their nation should be governed. In 1858 these tensions erupted into the Mexican War of Reform. The conflict was between the liberal and conservative groups. The US government felt the liberals would make better neighbors. So the United States sent aid to the liberal side. US soldiers were also allowed to join the liberal forces. In 1861 the liberals won the war.

As Mexico's civil war drew to a close, a war was beginning in the United States. The debate over slavery, which had helped stoke the fires of the Mexican-American War, still raged. The huge amount of land won by the United States in the war—and the question of whether slavery would be legal there—had heightened tensions further.

US lawmakers looked for ways to resolve the question. A proposed law called the Wilmot Proviso had been introduced in 1846 during the Mexican-American War. The proposal aimed to outlaw slavery in any territory gained through the war. Southern lawmakers voted it down. Another attempt to address the issue was the Compromise of 1850. This group of five laws passed in September 1850 gave both sides of the slavery debate things they wanted. California joined the nation as a free state, while New Mexico and Utah became territories whose residents could vote on the issue.

Yet these laws were not enough to bridge the deep divide. Between December 1860 and June 1861, eleven states in the South broke away from the United States over slavery and other disagreements with the North. They founded a new government called the Confederate States of America. The North was led by President Abraham Lincoln. It became known as the Union. Lincoln refused to accept the South's secession. The US Civil War began in April 1861. It ended in April 1865 with a victory for the North, but hundreds of thousands of people had died.

President Abraham Lincoln

Difficult Changes

Under Spanish and Mexican rule, American Indian nations had largely been able to live peacefully. While clashes did sometimes erupt between groups of native peoples and Mexican or US settlers, overall these nations had held onto much of their cultural and political independence.

US control of these lands would change that. US leaders encouraged US settlers to move onto lands that were home to native peoples. That settlement created conflicts and also displaced American Indians from their homes.

Many American Indians were pressured to assimilate or

move out of territory the United States had won in the Mexican-American War. In some cases, war broke out between US troops and native peoples, especially the Navajo and the Apache. Many American Indians were forced onto reservations, sometimes after grueling marches during which many people died.

Close Ties

Mexico's wars were not yet over. The Mexican Revolution (1910–1920) began when a group of rebels joined to overthrow President Porfirio Díaz. During and after the Mexican Revolution, nearly nine hundred thousand people immigrated to the United States to escape the violence. Most settled in Texas and other border states. They kept alive parts of their culture, language, and heritage. They formed strong communities, and they looked for work. But the new arrivals faced prejudice from white citizens. To combat this, a group of Hispanic immigrants founded the League of United Latin American Citizens in 1929. This civil rights group worked to fight discrimination.

That year the Great Depression (1929–1942) started. This serious economic downturn caused millions of people to lose their jobs.

President Porfirio Díaz

In response, the US government decided to deport some immigrants, as well as their descendants. This would free up jobs for other citizens. Between 1929 and 1939, the United States forced at least four hundred thousand Mexican immigrants and Mexican American citizens—and possibly more than one million—to leave the country.

During World War II (1939–1945), large numbers of US workers joined the military and went overseas to fight. Without them, US farms did not have enough labor. Meanwhile, many people in Mexico needed work. So in 1942, the US and Mexican governments agreed to start the Bracero Program, which brought Mexican farmworkers to the United States temporarily.

The Bracero Program lasted until 1964. During the program's twenty-two years, more than four million seasonal farmworkers traveled north to work on farms in California, Texas, and other states. But some farm owners insisted that braceros work very long, hard hours in exchange for very low pay.

To fight for better conditions, Cesar Chavez and Dolores Huerta founded the United Farm Workers (UFW) in 1962.

Cesar Chavez (*center*) walks with grape pickers to support the UFW.

This labor union worked to protect the rights of agricultural laborers in the United States. The UFW organized strikes demanding higher pay and better treatment.

Life in the United States could be difficult for Mexican immigrants. But many people who needed work were willing to take the risks. Some came to the United States without proper permission. Some US citizens were strongly opposed to the immigration of Mexican people. This tension continues to the present day.

Over the years, Mexico and the United States have not always seen eye to eye. But they share a nearly 2,000-mile (3,218 km) border, close economic ties, an overlapping history, and many families with members on both sides of the border. From the Mexican-American War to modern times, the histories and futures of Mexico and the United States remain tightly woven together.

In 2013 US president Barack Obama (*left*) and Mexican president Enrique Peña Nieto shake hands.

Writing Activity

Imagine that you are a soldier or a civilian in Mexico during the Mexican-American War. How would the conflict affect you? How would it affect your family? Your larger community? Your country?

Choose an event from one of the timelines that interests you. Imagine that you saw this event take place. Then write a journal entry about it. As you write, think about questions such as these:

How did you feel about the event?

What did you do in response to the event?

What surprised you most about this event?

Was your life different after this event?

What do you think the long-term effects of this event will be?

What is the most important thing you want to remember about this event?

Glossary

Catholicism: a branch of Christianity

civilian: a person who is not in the military

criollo: a person of Spanish descent who was born in Mexico

discrimination: unfair treatment of a person or a group of people

immigration: the process of moving to and settling in a new country

mestizo: a person living in Mexico who had mixed Spanish and native heritage

missionary: a religious worker. Missionaries often work to convert people to Christianity but may also build schools and do other community work.

prejudice: an idea or an opinion (often negative) that is not based on reason or actual experience

ratify: to approve a law or a treaty, usually by voting or signing a document

reservation: an area of land set aside by the US government for American Indians to live on

treaty: a written agreement between two or more parties

Further Information

DePietro, Frank. *Mexican Americans*. Philadelphia: Mason Crest, 2013. Learn more about the experiences and history of Mexican American people.

Duffield, Katy. *California History for Kids: Missions, Miners, and Moviemakers in the Golden State*. Chicago: Chicago Review, 2012. This book covers California history, from ancient times through its days as Mexican territory and beyond.

Hull, Robert. *The Aztec Empire*. New York: Gareth Stevens, 2011. Explore the history and culture of the Aztec people before the arrival of Europeans in lands that later became Mexico.

Texas Revolution
https://tshaonline.org/handbook/online/articles/qdt01
Find out more about the Texas Revolution in this article from *The Handbook of Texas Online*.

U.S.-Mexican War: 1846–1848
http://www.pbs.org/kera/usmexicanwar/index_flash.html
This PBS website includes interactive maps, biographies of important people, and more fascinating facts about the Mexican-American War.

Watson, Stephanie. *A Timeline History of the California Gold Rush*. Minneapolis: Lerner Publications, 2016. Learn more about the discovery of gold in California in January 1848, just one month before California became part of the United States as a result of the Mexican-American War.

LERNER
SOURCE

Expand learning beyond the printed book. Download free, complementary educational resources for this book from our website, www.lerneresource.com.

Index

Photo Acknowledgments

The images in this book are used with the permission of: The Granger Collection, New York, pp. 4–5, 22, 23; © DeAgostini/SuperStock, p. 8; © North Wind Picture Archives/Alamy, pp. 9, 15; © Niday Picture Library/Alamy, p. 10; © World History Archive/Alamy, p. 16; © Album/SuperStock, p. 20; Wikimedia Commons, pp. 21, 24; Library of Congress LC-USZC4-1642, p. 27; © De Agostini Picture Library/Bridgeman Images, p. 28; © Private Collection/Topham Picturepoint/Bridgeman Images, p. 30; © De Agostini Picture Library/G. Dagli Orti/ Bridgeman Images, p. 31; © Stock Montage, Inc./Alamy, p. 32; © Jesús Eloy Ramos Lara/Dreamstime.com, p. 33; © Laura Westlund/Independent Picture Service, p. 35; © Universal History Archive/UIG/Bridgeman Images, p. 37; © Archive Photos/Getty Images, p. 38; Library of Congress (LC-DIG-hec-10970), p. 40; Aurelio Escobar Castellanos, Archive/Wikimedia Commons (CC BY-SA 3.0), p. 41; © Arthur Schatz/The LIFE Picture Collection/Getty Images, p. 42; © Enrique Peña Nieto/flickr.com (CC BY-SA 2.0), p. 43.

Front cover: Wikimedia Commons.

Main text font set in Caecilia Com 55 Roman 11/16.
Typeface provided by Linotype AG.